JACK SIM presє

THE
GHOSTS
OF
BOGGO ROAD
GAOL

GHOSTS & GALLOWS

BY
JACK SIM

DEDICATION

To Don Walters,
the man responsible for Boggo Road Gaol still standing today.

& Alain Lewis,
who spent many years in prison with the ghosts...

Jack Sim

It is the intention of the publisher and author to present the material contained in this publication for historical and educational purposes only. There is no intention to defame individuals or deliberately cause grief to any person or persons associated with these stories. In certain circumstances some details have been removed to protect individuals rights to privacy. Every attempt has been made to procure original source material, including oral histories, however some records are not publicly available or have been lost. The publisher and author apologise for any incomplete material or offence caused.

Readers will note that all measurements and distances mentioned throughout the story are in the old imperial system. This was done to preserve the integrity of the statements as they were originally given, and to maintain a feeling for the atmosphere of the era in which the story is set. Every effort has been made to ensure that all historical material published is as accurate as possible.

First edition October 2008
Second edition November 2012
Third edition July 2013
Fourth edition September 2013 – 100th anniversary edition
Fifth edition June 2014
Sixth edition February 2015
This edition August 2015
Ghost Trails Series – www.ghosttrails.com.au

Jack Sim Publications
P O Box 1457
Sunnybank Hills Brisbane
Queensland 4109
www.jacksim.com.au

© 2015 Jack Sim

Sim, Jack 1971 -

THE GHOSTS OF BOGGO ROAD GAOL: Ghosts & Gallows.

Bibliography
ISBN 9780975796061

133.1099431

Printed by Cranbrook Press, Toowoomba, Queensland, Australia

C O N T E N T S

INTRODUCTION

This is the seventh reprint of THE GHOSTS OF BOGGO ROAD GAOL. It's hard to believe that this little book has sold more than 10,000 copies. It shows that interest in ghosts in this creepy old prison continues to thrill visitors and readers. This edition has been extended to 40 pages – and includes a wonderful poem from prison officer and poet George Carter about the ghost of the back track published for the first time!

The reputation that the most notorious prison in Australia in the Twentieth Century is haunted comes down to one person – me. From my mid-teens, like most people growing up in Brisbane, Boggo Road Gaol began to hold great interest. At that time the prison was living up to its reputation of being one of the most draconian, backward and vile prisons ever. A series of riots and escapes dominated the headlines and television screens. These were the last days of Boggo Road. In 2002, the doors of Boggo Road finally closed forever.

In January 1998 I tentatively walked up to the imposing gates of Number Two Division – the only section still standing of Boggo Road Gaol. I rapped on the gate, as visitors to this section of the prison had for over ninety years. I was greeted by a man with a thick Yorkshire accent who introduced himself as the curator of the Boggo Road Gaol Museum. Don Walters was an instantly likeable man whose forthrightness on the phone disappeared somewhat in person. Donny led me into his office inside the gatehouse of the gaol. We sat down at the table and he asked me did I have my insurance as requested over the phone, 'Yes', I replied, 'would you like to see it?'. 'No', he said, 'we have a gentleman's agreement'. With that he handed me a large ring with a huge set of keys to the front gates of Boggo Road Gaol.

Don Walters was employed by the Environment Department and the handover of keys came after I applied to the department to run historical tours at the site, including ghost tours. At that time my knowledge of the history of Boggo Road Gaol was limited, like most Brisbanites, to what I'd seen and read in the media. No institution, except perhaps our public hospitals, had affected more lives in Brisbane than had this place.

In the beginning Boggo Road was merely a small mainland holding prison. The main place for encarceration of long term sentenced men was St Helena Island in Moreton Bay. Over time the reputation of Boggo Road grew. By the end of the Twentieth Century it was without equal in Australia for brutality, horror and trouble. This prison had a bad beginning – a triple execution was held in 1883, soon after it opened. A Scotsman, and two aboriginal warriors – one a child – were simultaneously executed at the end of a rope by the hand of one of our State's best known executioners. In time many more offenders were despatched on the gallows of the gaol.

As the history of violence and horror grew inside the gaol becoming part of the culture of the surrounding community and the State, the media, first in newspapers then in radio broadcasts and eventually also television spread this knowledge. Few actual prisoners or prison guards, known as warders in Australia, spoke of what they had seen and experienced inside. Various myths and legends grew up about what went on behind those infamous red brick walls.

I was determined, right from the start, that I wanted to know the facts and the details – the truth behind the myths and legends. And as I researched I learned more and more about the history of the gaol. Through Don Walters I interviewed numerous former prison officers and prisoners; some of whom I now regard as very close and dear friends. I sat for literally hundreds of hours with total strangers who poured out to me their fabulous oral histories. I was the first person to take an interest in actually recording this material. Most of these men had never spoken to anyone other than colleagues before.

I learned of the killers, the murderers, the rapists; the child molestorers, the deviants, the thugs, the gunmen; the burglars, the escapologists, the riots, the protests, the strikes (they were few), the procedures, the routines, the rituals, the personalities, the staff and the ghost stories.

The reality is that the ghost stories of Boggo Road Gaol are few – despite the hype. Most of the creepy experiences had by officers and prisoners took place in very specific parts of the gaol. Many of these experiences did not have complex origins and indeed most of the time men were able to explain logically what it was they experienced – after all, would you want to let yourself become spooked while working in an infamous prison surrounded by desperate men who would take advantage of any weakness?

In 1998, when I began running my ghost tours, my intention was to bring to people the haunted heritage of the gaol. My tours, I am proud to say, were based entirely on the stories told to me by real people. I never made up a single yarn, or embellished a single story. My staff and I proudly told the tales that these men swapped among themselves while locked up, or released into the yards, or on night shift – stories which some of them had kept quiet throughout their entire careers. Many of them feared being ridiculed but were proud that a young man had taken an interest in their lives, and likewise I remain proud to have met some of the amazing people who survived imprisonment, whether as guards or prisoners, at Boggo Road Gaol.

This book is about those who did not survive, but linger still.

Until I started at Boggo Road Gaol there were no ghost tours of prisons anywhere in the world; now they are common. My tours have been copied at virtually any historic gaol you care to name - and I can ask for no greater compliment. I am proud that from Brisbane I was able to give knowledge of our most feared institution to the entire world. Read this book but do not share its content with others – what you will learn is privileged information passed from person to person by word of mouth. Some of these yarns are extremely old and come from the mouths of men now dead. It is through their experiences that you will learn of the ghosts of Boggo Road Gaol.

Jack Sim

NUMBER TWO DIVISION: The gothic entrance to one of the hardest prisons in Queensland.

Chapter 1

THE WARDER OF NUMBER TWO DIVISION

Most of the ghost stories of Boggo Road Gaol come from prison guards, known in Australia as "warders". It was guards on night shift, especially those on duty in old Number One Division – regarded as the most haunted section, who claimed to see the most ghosts.

In the old days, there were merely two sections to Boggo Road – Number One Division and Number Two Division, of which today only Number Two Division survives. During the day, dozens of unarmed officers performed various duties – releasing prisoners in the morning into the yards and then carrying out musters, escorting prisoners to their places of employment and various sections of the gaol, carrying out administration work, taking inmates to court and to hospital, and watching carefully prisoners in the workshops where criminals had easy access to materials they could use to escape or make weapons. Officers armed with rifles manned the towers on the walls of the gaol. At night however, only two officers patrolled the two sections of the prison on foot whilst locked up in the cell blocks that towered above them were hundreds of sleeping and desperate prisoners. Officers only carried revolvers at night.

These two officers were isolated from each other and only had keys to the sections they patrolled. It was common knowledge throughout the prison that they did not have keys to the cell blocks for if they did they would almost certainly have been killed for them.

Of the many ghost tales told by guards, the one most spoken about was that of a prison warder. Most stories of this spirit date to the 1970s and 1980s, the last decades of Boggo Road Gaol. Former officers today say that the origins of this ghost can be traced to a specific incident. On Monday, 7 March 1966, at 2.10pm, Bernard "Bernie" Ralph, aged fifty, devoted husband and father of three, was brutally attacked in the prison workshops. Warder Ralph, an Irishman, had worked at the prison for several years and was experienced at the job. He had been called in from his day off to work in the boot shop in Number Two Division. The permanent trade instructor in the boot shop was ill and Ralph was brought in to relieve him. It was not his usual role.

Ralph's killer was twenty-one year old John Hobson, a convicted murderer with an unpredictable nature. On Boxing Day 1961, Hobson, then a child aged seventeen, went berserk with a gun, killing three people and severely wounding another. He was sentenced to life imprisonment. Hobson, who was working in the boot shop, picked up an iron bar and walked up behind Ralph, who was sitting on a chair checking records. Warder Ralph never knew what hit him. Hobson, a dense giant with great strength, struck him twice on the head, severely fracturing his skull. Guards and inmates still speak of the horrific sight of the man's body lying in a pool of blood on the concrete floor of the boot shop, his head smashed in.

Hobson's motives for killing Ralph remain unclear, but it is likely he had been put up to this deed by another prisoner. Ralph was a strict officer, always ready to apply the regulations, and this apparently had made him unpopular with some inmates. Already serving life, Hobson had nothing to lose.

Ralph died in hospital from his extreme injuries. He remains to this day the only guard ever killed on duty in a Queensland prison.

Soon after Ralph's death, stories began that his ghost haunted Number Two Division. Officers at night claimed to have seen the apparition of a guard dressed in uniform walking as if on patrol. It was the presence of his spirit which was said to explain the unseen footsteps heard by guards at night. The figure was highly detailed, dressed in a prison uniform – hat, jacket, trousers and shoes. During research however, it became clear that no officers who had seen this ghost ever claimed to have recognised it as Warder Ralph. Interestingly men who knew him in life could not recall ever seeing the ghosts face. Indeed, research revealed that the story of a prison warder haunting the grounds seemed to pre-date the death of Bernard Ralph. The first stories of a ghostly guard begin in the 1930s. At that time, the figure seen was dressed in the uniform worn by prison guards in the 1900s; in the 1940s the prison guard ghost seen was dressed in the uniform of the 1920s; in the 1960s the ghost was dressed in the 1940s style of tunic; from the 1970s and 1980s the ghost is described as being that of Warder Ralph but it is clear that this tale existed before his murder. No one ever mentions a face.

Guards on track duty describe a figure walking towards them who would stop, raise its hand to its head and salute making them believe it was the Night Senior – the senior officer on duty at the prison overnight who would routinely sneak about the prison to ensure that officers were on duty and not asleep at their post. Officers would jump to attention, salute back and say, 'Post present and correct sir.' The Senior would then continue on his patrol. But when the ghost of the Warder was seen it would merely salute back, say nothing, and then continue on its way. Sometimes passing very close, within a foot or so of the officer, without saying a word, its footsteps continued to be heard crunching in the gravel of the track long after it had disappeared from view.

One night in the 1970s when an officer named Don Walters was on duty he unexpectedly saw the Night Senior standing on the track ahead of him. He saluted his superior who responded with a salute but said nothing and walked past him. In the morning when Don finished his shift he asked the gate officer whether John Lennon had been on duty the previous night; he was told that Mr Lennon (not the rock star, but an officer at the prison) could not have been because he was on leave at the Gold Coast with his family.

* * *

In December 1975 prison officers unveiled a memorial at the prison to Bernard Ralph. A photograph of him was put on the wall of the Officer's Mess as a tribute to him. Despite all officers taking their meals in this room none of those that saw the ghost of the Warder ever mentioned the spirit as having his face.

Ralph's poor wife never received any compensation for her husband's death, despite many years of trying. The State refused to admit any responsibility and indeed placed the blame for his death on his failure to wear a regulation helmet.

There is every reason why Bernard Ralph's ghost would haunt Number Two Division of Boggo Road Gaol – but I do not think that it is him. The ghost that is seen probably pre-dates him. There have been numerous deaths of staff, mostly of natural causes – it could be one or all of these. Ghosts can be an amalgamation of souls. John Hobson too died inside the walls of prison, dropping dead of a heart attack after years of strong medication to keep his violent tendencies at bay. If any spirit haunts the gaol it would be nice if it was his. Unfortunately there has never been any story of his ghost ever having been seen.

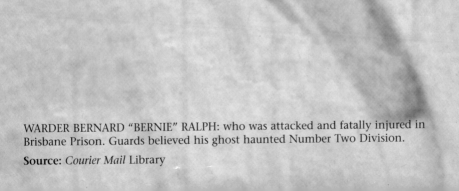

WARDER BERNARD "BERNIE" RALPH: who was attacked and fatally injured in Brisbane Prison. Guards believed his ghost haunted Number Two Division.

Source: *Courier Mail* Library

3

Chapter 2

THE GALLOWS

Between 1883 and 1913, thirty-nine men, one woman and two children were executed on the gallows at Boggo Road Gaol - then known officially as the Brisbane Gaol. The method used was hanging. The gallows created the most ghosts at Boggo Road.

The gallows were located on the first floor, above the entrance, of A Wing, the middle cellblock in the oldest section of the gaol - the section which would later become known as Number One Division. A set of stone stairs led up to the gallows from the ground floor. A cell was set aside for the condemned person.

The gallows consisted of a strong timber beam running across the breadth of the cellblock set deep into the walls. Three hooks hung beneath the beam to which the rope could be attached. A metal trapdoor formed the floor beneath the beam.

At eight o'clock on a Monday morning, a bell would toll to announce the grim act about to take place. A prisoner, hands secured by leather manacles, was led to the gallows accompanied by a priest. He or she would stand on the trapdoors directly below the beam. The executioner would pinion their feet with leather belts. This was to stop movement as the body resisted death.

The prisoner would face towards the window at the far end of the cellblock. The rays of the morning sun could sometimes be seen. The executed came from all over the world - Europe, England, Scotland, Ireland, Malaysia, China, Japan, the South Sea Islands. Many were aboriginal. They all had very different ideas of the afterlife, and what happened to those who committed murder, or who died innocent, or died violently. Some found Christ at the end, prayed to Allah, or to a god or gods. Several had no idea what awaited them and others were terrified of going to hell or being damned. Then they would say their last words. Some spoke little, some a lot. Some were angry, most were repentant. Some died brave, some cowards. One or two cried. One fainted. All would die.

Their piece said, the hangman would put a white, cloth hood over the prisoner's head. When a person is hanged, their eyes pop out of their head and their tongue protrudes out their mouth. It is a horrific sight. There was also a belief that a person could escape their punishment by sending their soul into the body of another through the eyes. This belief, and the desire to spare the official witnesses and the media present such a shocking sight was the reason for the hood.

The noose was then put around the person's neck, the knot placed exactly over the spine at the back of the neck so that the sudden jerk would break the spinal cord. In theory this would cause instantaneous death but in practice many did not die straight away, their hearts beating long after. Several had their throats cut; one had his head pulled off.

At a signal, the hangman would move a lever which opened the trap doors and sent the prisoner to eternity. A black flag was run up the prison's flagpole to indicate that the deed was done. After a doctor determined they were dead, the executed were put into pine coffins and taken away for burial at South Brisbane Cemetery, accompanied by a team of prisoners carrying picks and shovels.

Not only was the process a brutal way to die - always a great way to create tormented spirits - but it was also believed that the souls of those who committed such offences would be denied access into heaven. Theirs was an eternal punishment. In the cemetery they were buried in unmarked graves, to be forgotten and unlamented. The section in which they were buried was unconsecrated. There was genuine fear of these souls because of the evil they did, the way they died and that they may return seeking revenge on the living.

* * *

Witnesses were haunted for many years by the experience. Few present were immune to feelings of revulsion, horror and disgust. Prisoners who resided in A Wing, lived in the shadow of the gallows. They were removed from their cells during the deed, and were placed in the yards. To placate them they were issued tobacco. Warders were often sick afterwards; officials were issued stiff drinks after the body was removed.

Some wrote of the experience in journals, diaries and even literature. Reporters recorded every gruesome detail for eager readers keen to know that justice was done. Illustrators brought the work of "Jack Ketch" (the nickname for the executioner) into the houses of Brisbanites. One witness, Arthur Hoey Davis, was Sheriff's Officer and officiated at a hanging on behalf on the government. The impact did not stop him becoming Steele Rudd, one of Australia's most famous authors, of "On Our Selection".

The Gallows' end came in 1922 when Queensland became the first state in the British Empire to abandon capital punishment.

The Trap was welded up in the early 1930s so it could no longer be used. But at night in old A Wing, prisoners swore that the clang of the trap could still be heard.

Left: GRUESOME SCENE AT THE SCAFFOLD: Two warders lower the cadaver of the executed criminal through the Trap. The undertaker and executioner guide it into a coffin.

Source: *The Truth,* Sunday, 20 May 1906 page 5

Right: THE HANGMAN ADJUSTS THE ROPE: Witnesses watch as a priest reads from the Bible as the hangman secures the noose around the neck of the man condemned to die.

Source: *The Truth,* Sunday, 23 July 1905 page 5

7

GALLOWS BEAM

MANY NOTED CRIMINALS WERE HANGED ON THIS BEAM AT BOGGO ROAD JAIL BRISBANE

Above: THE GALLOWS BEAM: in storage in the Queensland Museum vaults. The three hooks to which the executioner would attach his rope can be seen. This macabre relic must be returned permanently to Boggo Road Gaol.

Source: Author's own collection.

Right: THE GALLOWS: a rare photgraph of the scaffold in A Wing (now demolished).

Source: State Library (Queensland)

Wing sweepers – the last prisoners to be locked up at night – tried to solve the mysterious noise by placing used matches on the trap – only to find them broken on the floor in the morning. By the 1940s a strange tradition emerged among guards – they would dance on the disued trap, mainly as a joke, to kind of laugh in the face of death.

Officially it was in 1956 that the gallows were dismantled. But former guards say they were responsible for its removal in the 1970s, just prior to the demolition of old A Wing. They souvenired it...

A piece of the Trap, on which the worst criminals in Queensland history stood moments before their death at the end of a rope, became the cooking plate of a family barbeque on the north side of Brisbane.

The bolt from the door of the condemned man's cell also survived, along with the wooden box in which the executioner stored his ropes, straps and other grisley equipment.

The Beam was sawn down and the end pieces cut up into blocks with a chainsaw. Warders took bits home - much to the horror of their wives, who soon saw to it that these macabre chunks of history were consigned to the garage or even the tip. The largest section spent many years on display at Newstead House, before being put into storage in the Queensland Museum. At present it resides in the collection of the Royal Historical Society of Queensland. This macabre relic must be returned permanently to Boggo Road Gaol.

GHOST STORY

HAUNTED BY PHANTOM CRIMINALS: The unhappy hangman
flees from the ghosts of the sixteen people he put to death.

Source: *The Truth,* Sunday, 19 November 1905 page 5.

Chapter 3

THE HAUNTED HANGMAN

Why Sam Hudson chose to become the hangman of Boggo Road Gaol is unknown. It couldn't have been for the money. Before he took the job Hudson ran a successful business as a village blacksmith. Aged in his late forties, Hudson possessed a powerful, muscular build. Hudson put to death some of this State's most infamous murderers including Patrick Kenniff, Australia's last bushranger. In all he executed sixteen individuals and was the longest-serving executioner at Boggo Road.

Whereas the previous hangman was unreliable, Hudson was an expert man-killer – responsible, civic minded, steady – an artist of death. He did the deed which no-one else would or wanted to. His cheery personality earned him a nickname in the press – "Happy Hangman Hudson". By November 1905 he was sick of the job. He resigned. The government was furious.

Initially paid an annual salary of £125 ($250) as well as an allowance of five pounds ($10) for every execution – not a large amount given what he was required to do, Hudson became unhappy when the Government stopped paying the allowance. Further, the State Government did not seem to care about his personal safety. On a number of occasions he was attacked by thugs; it was merely his strength and ability to fight that saved him.

There was another reason why he quit - the ghosts of those he despatched started coming back to haunt him:

> Though he hides from the sight of his fellow men, he cannot escape from the uncanny vision, the abominable apparitions which ever and anon haunt him. One moment the black, agonising form of a Kanaka's face will conjure up in his diseased imagination, followed with lightning-like rapidity by a fellow white-man's contemptuous stare until the whole 16 of his victims, armed with the dreaded noose, manacles, and tools of his degrading profession, would seem to be crowding in upon him, hissing their curses in his livid face. These chasing phantoms are too much for him.

Relentlessly pursued by the newspapers who wanted to publish his photograph, having to burn his clothes which became soaked with blood, forced to wear a disguise and only travel at night, fearful for his wife and family's safety, Hudson turned to spirits to ease his troubled mind. He would have a glass of brandy before the execution and afterwards, avoiding the press, he would sit alone in a cell and drink the whole bottle. He lost friends, his business and community respect: 'damned and despised by all who know what I am, like a "moral leper"'.

The now haunted hangman, decided to leave the country. Bound by contract to work until the end of the year, Hudson put his wife on a ship to America. The State Government, fearful their faithful servant slayer would flee too, sinisterly sent a detective to overshadow him at the wharves and at all times.

When his obligations finally expired, after he had trained his replacement, Hudson followed his wife to San Francisco, in the United States, to escape the ghosts which tormented him and filled his dreams. Hudson had aged dramatically; he had lost his hair and his powerful frame was reduced to a stoop. According to rumour, he shot himself a few weeks after arriving in the new world.

C WING CELLBLOCK, NUMBER TWO DIVISION. Prisoners in the 1980s claimed the ghost of

Chapter 4

A BANSHEE WAILED –
THE LAST MAN HANGED

A prison officer, known to the author, was told the story when he started work at Boggo Road in 1935, that the ghost of the last man executed haunted the prison. The man's body was supposed to lie buried behind A Wing, which housed the gallows, in one of the yards.

The last prisoner executed was in 1913. Twenty-two years later, a very creepy ghost tale had taken deep root among guards and prisoners alike. There are many different versions. Each and every teller has his own tale. Never the less, it became the oldest and most enduring ghost story told within the walls of the prison.

* * *

The Mitchell family were concerned. Dusk had fallen and their lovely daughter and sister, Ivy Alexandra Mitchell, eleven years of age, had not yet returned home. She had spent the day playing with friends at their farm several miles away. The Mitchell's lived at Samford – a rural community North-West of Brisbane. Mr Mitchell and his son began a search for her. Near the state school that she attended they found her bare footprints and beside them another set of tracks produced by large boots. The tracks led off into dense scrub opposite. The Mitchell's followed them into the bush.

The light of their hurricane lantern revealed a scene straight from hell. Little Ivy's body lay in a pool of blood. Her head had been nearly severed from her neck. The bunch of flowers that Ivy had been carrying in her hand, and a packet of sweets lay broken on the ground beside her. It was clear that Ivy had struggled and screamed but her cries had gone unheard. Only a monster could commit such an act.

The next morning a young man was led to the scene of the crime, where Ivy's body still lay. His boots matched the tracks. As the white sheet covering her cold body was drawn back, he merely glanced at her and lied, 'I don't know her'.

Ernest Austin, twenty-three years old, a farmhand who worked on the Mitchell's property was charged with murder. Employed by the girl's father to perform farm work, he had often played with young Ivy, picking flowers together.

After six hours deliberation, the jury delivered their verdict. The Chief Justice sentenced Austin to 'be hanged by the neck until you are dead and may the Lord have mercy on your soul'.

On Monday, 22 September, 1913 as the bell within the gatehouse tolled three times, in a time honoured tradition, prisoners in A Wing, who lived in the shadow of the gallows, were led out of the cell block and into the yards on either side. There they were given tobacco to placate them whilst they listened to the terrible act about to be played out within the walls of their home.

A few minutes later, Ernest Austin was led from the cell reserved for condemned criminals to the gallows.

He did not hesitate and walked firmly to stand in the centre of the trapdoors, facing those on the floor of the gallery:

> Austin speaking in a firm voice, said: 'I ask my mother to forgive me... God save the King!' In his last moments he asked that a "wire" be sent to his mother telling her that 'he died happy and without fear'.

> The white cap was drawn over his face and, at a sign, the executioner pulled the lever. At exactly eight o'clock the hangman did his work. Death was instantaneous.

Long-term prisoners tell a different version of Austin's last words. They say that under the influence of a shot of morphine Austin started to laugh just as the trap doors opened beneath him. All the way to the end of the rope he laughed madly, and even then tried to force out one last little chuckle from between his lips.

It was said that the laughter as he fell was often heard in the early mornings in the cellblocks. But even more frightening was the belief that on dark stormy nights, as heavy rain beat down upon the tin roof of A Wing in old Number One Division, Austin would return from the grave. He would materialise from the white painted wall at the front of A Wing, the very cellblock in which he had been executed, and he would begin a slow pace of the ground floor, passing cells until he found one which contained his victim. He would stop outside the cell door and rap three times. If the ghost heard any sound it would pass through the door and strangle the inmate.

Austin had done a deal with the devil; Satan gave him a chance to make it to the afterlife. If Austin brought him a set quota of souls, he will be released from Hell. The scary part was no one but Austin and the Devil knew how many souls were needed. The last man hung may still walk the gantries of the prison in search of one last victim...

In the 1950s the tale was made a full page feature in a popular Brisbane newspaper. Readers were chilled of the account of how a "Banshee Wailed" at Boggo Road. A banshee is a tormented spirit in Irish folklore, usually female, who screams to foretell the death of someone near. Almost certainly this story reinforced the existing beliefs of prisoners and guards that there was something in the tale:

> Shrill and stunningly sudden... supernatural perhaps, was the cry which penetrated, like an arrow, the heavy, brooding calm which prevailed in the execution yard of Brisbane Prison on the morning of September 22, 1913, as Ernest Austin – the last man to be hanged in Queensland – was about to hurtle to his doom through a gallows trapdoor.

> It was, perhaps, the screech of a bird; perhaps it was the cry of a child hurt at play in a nearby yard... or, perhaps, it was a spiritual shriek from beyond the grave – a spine-chilling ethereal acknowledgement that Austin's little girl victim was being avenged and Justice was being done.

> At all events, to those press-men and gaol officials whose grim duty it was to witness the execution, the cry, which echoed and re-echoed through the penitentiary while Austin stood on the scaffold, was the most nerve-racking and perplexing emotion it is possible for a man to experience.

> Various explanations were put forward in the press at the time to account for the phenomenon, but the question remained: Was it bird? Or child? Or the departed victim of a fiendish murderer's lust?

> Just before the hangman was ready to pull the lever – to the horror and amazement of those present at the hanging – "there was an awful cry of despair from the passage of the prison in which the hanging took place" so a chronicler of the scene reported at the time. Austin, who also heard that piercing cry, swayed on the scaffold trap-door and trembled violently. Nobody could account for the amazing shriek which virtually interrupted the execution. The hangman was considerably unnerved by the sound, and Austin, with rope round his neck, seemed about to fall in a faint when the masked executioner released the trap.

9415

E. Austin

Perhaps every victim who had seen justice done on those gallows cried out in triumph as the last man hung went to his fate. Or was it all the others that had gone before Austin? That had ended others lives, and so had theirs ended too? Knowing that he was the last, they screamed out to welcome him. Austin was doomed... He would soon be theirs... And both he knew and they knew it.

* * *

In 1979, the year that another infamous character - John Stuart - would die in Boggo, a local newspaper under the title "So Much Hot Air" revealed how well known the ghost story was inside the prison:

> At 8 am on September 22, 1913, inside Boggo Road Jail, a young farm labourer named Ernest Austin was hanged on the prison gallows.
>
> Hardly a nourishing thought over Sunday breakfast, but Septimus has a good reason and Mr. Austin is certainly in no position to care.
>
> It is his "ghost" that is now reported to be scaring the stripes out of the jail's younger guests and a few of their keepers.
>
> But the "super" at Boggo, Bob Smith, a pretty religious bloke himself, last week "buried" Ernie's ghost for good.
>
> "It's too silly for words," he said. "Every couple of years some old wag tells a young prisoner that if he looks at the wall in A Wing, where the gallows used to be, he'll see the famous jail ghost on a dark blustery night.
>
> "Of course he'll see the wavering reflection from one of the prison lights blowing in the breeze,
>
> "We mightn't have the most modern prison in Australia – yet – but we don't scrimp in electricity."
>
> It was amazing, concluded Smithy, how many prisoners were prepared to "buy" the tale.
>
> It had added impetus with the knowledge that murderer Ernie Austin was the last bloke hanged in Queensland and his "ghost" is a bit dirty on that.

By the 1980s, old A Wing, where the gallows had been, was demolished yet this did not end the ghost story of Ernest Austin. By this time the oldest surviving section of Boggo Road was Number Two Division. E Wing cellblock became the new location for the ghost story of Ernest Austin. Inmates held there during the eighties, like their predecessors over the last half century, also lay in their cells at night terrified that "Ernie" would come to get them. It seems this ghost was determined to survive in the minds of men.

Since 1998 Ghost Tours have operated historic tours of Boggo Road. Whilst it can be said that the creepiness of the site lends itself to overactive imaginations, both clients and staff have since that time claimed to have seen the silhouette of a man standing on the upper floors, at the top of the stairs, in E Wing cellblock, and even seen it beneath the stairs on the ground floor as if coming out of the back wall. This cell block is the same one that prisoners in the eighties claimed that Austin's spirit was seen.

Whether the ghost of Austin is real, or whether the story only exists in the minds of men, the story is now Australia's oldest prison ghost tale. Since that shriek echoed through A Wing in 1913 until now, 100 years later, the monster that was the last man hanged has haunted those who spend time in Boggo Road. It is a marvellous piece of haunted heritage and it is bloody chilling.

LOCATION OF GRAVES?: The yards at the back of A Wing, Number One Division. The back wall of A Wing can be seen at top of photograph. The verandah from which an officer saw a shape float above the yards can be seen running along the top of the wall. Number One Division no

Chapter 5

THE GRAVES...

It was rumoured that in the old days not all those executed on the prison gallows were buried at the South Brisbane Cemetery. Since 1883, the year the prison opened, those murderers and killers hung from the neck until dead were interred in unconsecrated earth in the swampiest part of that public burial ground. There was at least one, it was said, whom had been buried under one of the exercise yards at the back of A Wing, one of the three cellblocks of Number One Division, that which contained the gallows.

It was known that the door at the rear of the cellblock which led out into one of the yards was to allow for the prompt removal of the corpse after execution. There was a strong belief that the souls of these individuals were damned, and their remains should be disposed of quickly.

One story had it that it was the body of the last man to be hung in Queensland that lay beneath the feet of the prisoners during the day.

It was this story that was offered to explain the numerous sightings of ghosts and spirits at the back of Number One Division. There were many, many stories such as the sighting of a ghost in the early 1970s when an officer walking along the verandah at the back of A Wing saw a shape like a sheet float above the wall of one of the yards.

In the early 1980s when water pipes were being laid in the exercise yards of new Number One Division, contractors cutting deep into the ground noticed that in the walls of the channel they had cut, there were what appeared to be eight blackened pits. Guards overseeing the work were concerned. Quicklime, white when applied, turns black with the passage of time. Quicklime was poured over bodies to ensure rapid decomposition. A closer inspection revealed that embedded in the soil were pieces of cloth – the sacking that the dead were buried in? Immediately the workers, on full pay, downed tools, many of them fearful that they had disturbed graves – frightened that they may have unleashed evil spirits to return to the living...

They refused to work until the soil was tested. Allegedly scientists from the University of Queensland arrived at the scene the next day. They took soil samples and a long, thin bone that they had found in the bottom of the hole. The results on the soil were conclusive – these had been graves. The digging machine had apparently cut right through the middle of eight individuals buried within the walls of the former prison (the number of graves varies from storyteller to storyteller).

But the bone revealed a different result – it was not human. It was determined to be a fresh lamb bone. It seems that one of the warders, Ron Darby, the resident prankster and storyteller, took a lamb bone and threw it in the bottom of the hole. His motivation was simple – officers got paid for a week to stand around and guard a hole. Heads were supposed to roll, however somehow the officer who played the joke managed to avoid being reprimanded.

Extensive archaeology carried out in the mid–2000's revealed no trace of the graves, if there ever were any. It is unlikely that the grave or graves in this story were those of executed prisoners. It is more likely that these were victims of disease or plague but old warders cannot be convinced of this.

THE TUNNEL : as unearthed in 2006 by the Queensland State Government. Lost for more than

Chapter 6

THE TUNNEL OF LOVE

Stretching 120 feet (37 metres) in the cold, dark earth of Boggo Road Gaol was what was known as the tunnel. Built in the 1920s this underground passageway connected Number One Division or "One Jail" as it was also known with Number Two Division or "Two Jail". In the early 1920s prisoners had to be escorted from one section to the other out in the open from gatehouse to gatehouse. Following a series of escapes the decision was made to build this lengthy tunnel to escape-proof the prison.

At the time that the tunnel was constructed new workshops were erected at the rear of Number Two Division. The tunnel granted access to these. Each day prisoners were escorted by guards through the tunnel to the workshops where they would learn and carry out various trades. There was a gate at either end of the tunnel. A guard would walk ahead of the party of inmates and unlock the middle gate, proceed through to the other side, and then prisoners would be sent through. Guards tell of how cold and creepy it was. At its lowest point the tunnel was nine feet (3 metres) underground, and though kept painted and clean it still felt isolated and there was a chill in the air. It was the highlight of inmate's days to either march to work through the tunnel or to be returning to the relative safety of their cells along this route.

By the late 1960s, nearly half a century after it was built, the tunnel had attracted various legends among guards and prisoners which claimed the tunnel to be haunted. Prisoners gave this eerie passageway the nickname "The Tunnel of Love". Years ago at the Brisbane Exhibition, and at some traveling fairs, a popular attraction of the time was The Tunnel of Love. Couples would sit side by side in a float and would pass through an attraction depicting romantic scenes. It was, basically, an opportunity to kiss and canoodle without being seen. It was a great way for a man to make his intentions towards a woman known. The Tunnel of Love at Boggo Road Gaol was also the way in which a man made his intentions known. Young prisoners and youthful new arrivals would feel the rough hand of an older male prisoner grab theirs as they walked through the tunnel. If that was not terrifying enough, the stories told by the "old hand" would really chill them.

The explanation for the icy cold atmosphere and the freezing air current that flowed down through the tunnel and came out of the wall as you walked along its length to the other side was said to be the prisoners who were taken from Number Two Division to be executed on the gallows located in old Number One Jail. After their execution the ghosts of these prisoners lingered in the tunnel, retracing their final steps towards their doom. It was the souls of the executed dead coming out of the earth to get you.

The young prisoner would squeeze the older man's hand back, hence the nickname the Tunnel the Love, the closest thing to romance in Boggo Road. It is total bunkum that condemned prisoners ever walked this route. The last execution was in 1913, ten years before the tunnel was even built. Number Two Division itself was not built until 1903 and no prisoner ever executed was *ever* held there. Still, it's a great story.

D WING CELLBLOCK, NUMBER TWO DIVISION: This cellblock contained long term sentenced
prisoners and difficult cases. Night cans can be seen lined up outside each cell.

Chapter 7

THE CELLS

Prisoners could spend up to fourteen hours in the cellblocks of Boggo Road. Many preferred to be locked up than to be among other prisoners, safe from the bashings and trouble that were a regular part of daily life.

Today the cellblocks of Number Two Division are the only ones that survive. In use for eighty-six years, they were originally used to hold female prisoners; each contains forty-two cells. They ceased to be used for prisoners in 1989, just two decades ago. Even during the day, these cellblocks are eerie. Little light penetrates inside. The cells were always stinking hot in summer and freezing cold in winter. Prisoners had little furniture – a cell table, a stool, a mat, a canvas hammock and two grey woollen blankets. There was no running water. The toilet was a steel tub. Electric lights were turned off each night.

Official records, newspaper articles and documents can establish that over 100 people died within the walls of the gaol, including those executed there. A small number were murdered. Many others died of natural causes, sickness and illness. Some died of old age. A number died by their own hand. Prisoners taunted new arrivals with threats to encourage them to kill themselves. It is a sad fact that some inmates ended their lives out of shame and desperation. Pieces of metal and wire were used to cut wrists and throats. Determined inmates used their leather belt or would make a rope by plaiting together blankets cut into strips. They would soak the rope in their own urine to reduce the amount the wool would stretch. After tying the rope to the bars above the door to their cell, they would step off their toilet tub to strangle against the door.

There was no more haunting experience for a guard than to find a prisoner dead in a cell. The sight was never something they wanted to remember. Several tell of the unusual ways that bodies were found. One recalled a prisoner found sitting upright, facing towards the door, as if waiting for someone to come through. Another remembered how some clearly did not want to die at the end, and tried at the last to save themselves, but failed. One prisoner was found in A Wing in old Number One Div, dead, under his woolen blankets, still in his hammock. When the blanket was pulled back, the inmate's face was frozen in fear, his hands up near his chin, almost clutching at something. The cause of his death was not obvious; there were no signs that it was suicide. A post mortem revealed the man, aged in his early twenties, had died of a heart attack.

There was a cell on the ground floor of E Wing, Number Two Division, in which a prisoner was found hanging. The guard that found him swore that every time he opened the door to the cell he'd feel the dead weight of a body on it, years after the incident.

Indigenous prisoners were particularly sensitive and would refuse to be put into those cells where they could feel men had taken their lives. They would demand to be moved stating 'there's been dead white fella in here. He's still in here', or that there were 'bad spirits' inside. A cell in which an aboriginal person had died could not be used until it had been smoked clean of their spirit. Elders were brought in from outside to burn gum leaves and drive the lost spirit away.

Chapter 8

CELL F2

Warders and prisoners claimed that certain cells were haunted. Over time the exact location of most of these cells has been lost. To pin-point the exact location of cells in which people died, let alone supposedly haunt, is not only difficult, but too macabre to explore in print. But there were a number of cells that were known to have a "feeling" in them, that of a presence, like someone was in them. Some cells repeatedly came up over and over again. Prisoners claimed to feel and even see ghosts in them.

A "lifer" once told me that the real "ghosts" in prison are the ghosts of your own past. At night, alone in a cell, inmates think about the things they did to put themselves inside. These ghosts could kill you...if you let them.

* * *

In 1947 the monotony of gaol life in Number Two Division was broken by the protestations of a loud-mouth. A prisoner, on remand for murder, irritated all and sundry by constantly crowing about his innocence. No one in prison is guilty of anything. I am yet to meet a single guilty prisoner. But, if there is one thing men serving life hate, it is someone who won't shut up about his innocence - especially when they know that he's good for it.

Day in, day out they listened to this man tell them how he had nothing to do with the murder of his eighteen year old secretary and that he had been the victim of a conspiracy. The vivacious teenager with many friends and suitors was choked to death by her boss in their mutual workplace. He then stripped her of clothing and tried to make it appear that she had committed suicide. Despite overwhelming evidence against him he maintained throughout the trial an indifference towards what he had done, showed no remorse, and claimed that anyone who committed crimes like murder should hang. Until he was sentenced Brown was confident that he would be vindicated. He believed his own lies to the very end.

After his trial, once he had been found guilty, Brown proved to be a man of his word. Brown had been placed in what was then an observation cell – Cell F2, cell number two in F Wing cellblock. Brown attached his belt to the bars above the door and made a noose out of a couple of knotted handkerchiefs.

Why Brown was left with his prison issue belt remains a mystery; prisoners about to begin their sentences were stripped of anything that they might use to kill themselves. Brown was found dangling against the door early the next morning. It is said that when the Superintendent was advised at breakfast time of the discovery he replied, 'Let the bastard hang'.

When the body was cut down, in his shirt pocket was found a suicide note. It was written on lavatory paper in neat handwriting: 'I did not kill that girl'. Even at the end he could not admit his guilt.

For the next forty years prisoners put in this cell maintained that on certain nights you could hear the sound of leather stretching in the vicinity of the door and the sound of the heels of a pair of shoes tapping against it as a ghostly body swung in its death throws and banged against it.

C TOWER, NUMBER TWO DIVISION: Scene of unique experiences, including a ghost whom

Chapter 9

THE TOWERS

The stark white Bessa Block walls of the new Brisbane Prison, constructed in the 1970s. contrasted dramatically against the old red brick walls of Number Two Division. The new prison, whose infamous inmates included Johnny Stuart and James Finch (the Whiskey Au Go Go nightclub bombers), would, by the 1980s, develop the notoriety of Boggo Road even more – through riots, strikes and a series of spectacular escapes.

Walkways ran along the top of the walls of this new complex connecting the Towers. Soon after the new Brisbane Prison opened, guards began claiming that they saw officers and unidentifiable figures striding along the catwalks and gantries. Some of these figures carried guns. One fellow who had seen ghosts night after night, eventually refused to work there anymore. His replacement didn't believe in ghosts either, but it the middle of the night, his phone rang. Each guard tower had a telephone allowing communication between the towers, the main gate and administration. When the officer picked up the phone, it was silent. Twice more it rang; twice it was silent. At first he thought this must have been a prank; but after it occurred several more times on different shifts he became convinced that something rather than someone was trying to communicate with him. Several other officers during the 1980s also experienced the strange phone calls.

Ghosts were also blamed for other problems with communication. Despite being a state-of-the-art penitentiary, technical problems seemed to plague electronic equipment. Some maintain that the prison was a gigantic white elephant - poorly built and poorly run. It was the living who could be blamed for its faults, not the dead.

***

For nearly ninety years, the presence of a guard in C Tower, the turret visible from Annerley Road, has reassured residents living near the prison. Each morning an officer and a Senior would proceed to the steel door at the base of the tower. After unlocking it with a key, the officer on tower duty would ascend the spiral staircase inside to the top. There he would lower the key on a string down to the Senior who would lock him in. The guard would pull up the string and he would spend the rest of his shift up in the tower with one of the finest views in Brisbane. The tower had its own toilet – not that it was used much. Officers who sat on the throne reckoned that ghostly footsteps could be heard on the staircase right beside the toilet. Plenty of officers reckoned they'd 'sooner piss themselves' than meet the source of those footsteps whilst sitting down.

Like those in Number One Division, the tower on the wall of Two Division was never manned at night; but generations of locals and many prison guards on track duty inside the walls swear to have seen a guard with a rifle slung over his shoulder walking backwards and forwards along the catwalk.

Not knowing that the tower was unmanned at night a local resident wrote to the Superintendent of the prison in 1973, thanking him for improving security by finally installing a guard at that post. It is my understanding that the letter was never answered.

GHOST STORY

THE SOUTHERN WALL OF NUMBER TWO DIVISION: Over this wall came the cemetery fog.
Source: Author's own collection.

Chapter 10

THE CEMETERY FOG

Many weird phenomena were observed by warders at night on track duty at Number Two Division. There were a lot of stories of strange fogs and mists that would appear floating over the yards or be seen in the distance right at the end of the track, that would float around the corner and disappear from sight. The sensible would say that this used to happen the most around 4.00am just before daybreak, when you were at your most tired. They reckoned that these sightings were not ghosts, just tricks of the light caused by tired eyesight.

The Cemetery Fog was different. It seemed to only occur following rain or on cold nights. One of those to see it was Don Walters, who later became the curator at Boggo Road Gaol. It was one of his favourite stories to tell.

It was different and genuinely creepy. This thick, white, curling fog would be observed rolling over the top of the southern wall of Number Two Division, right beside C Tower (or Three Tower as the tower on the wall, seen from Annerley Road was later known). The fog, like something from an old Hammer Horror film, would cascade down the wall like a slowly flowing waterfall. When it reached the track, officers ran.

It would slowly form into two waves that would roll slowly down the track towards the guard. Guards in the know would run into the sentry box, lock the door, seal the cracks and gaps, and close the glass louvers. You see, if you let the drifting pale 'tendricals' of fog touch you, a freezing chill would pass through your very bones...within weeks you would be terribly ill, racked by pneumonia or at the least bronchitis. It was claimed that this fog brought disease with it, over the wall.

Why did they call it the Cemetery Fog? From the tower it could be seen coming up over the hill from the local graveyard, Dutton Park Cemetery. Prisoners who died in custody were 'released to Dutton Park' that is, buried in an unmarked grave in South Brisbane (Dutton Park) Cemetery. Many believed that those who died while serving a sentence were doomed to remain trapped forever within the gaol. The fog brought the souls of these poor prisoners back to their place of eternal torment.

* * *

Don Walters had another eerie experience. One night, on patrol, he found a firehose had unravelled itself. Such equipment was always kept neat and tidy, ready for use. The stranger part was that the full length of the hose was pointing straight up into the air, like the old Indian rope trick. Don tried to pull it down but it would not budge. Another officer was witness to the bizarre experience. Despite examining every possibility – that it was stuck on something or it was a prank, they could not account for it. Instead, they decided they would keep it to themselves rather than endure the heckles of others if they told of it or be considered mad or worse unfit, for the job.

GHOST STORY

TRIPOD IN LIFE: Prisoners jokingly referred to him as a "lifer" after 16 years of being in Boggo Road. The animal's spirit is said to still haunt the gaol.

Source: *Courier Mail* Library

Chapter 11

TRIPOD THE GHOST CAT

There were many animals inside the walls of Boggo Road Gaol, not all of them human.

Mice, cats and birds were all kept by inmates as pets. While not officially allowed they were tolerated. Prisoners trained mice and cockroaches to run messages between their cells; prisoners kept mice in their pockets, and even little birds. The most famous bird owner was James Finch, one of the two men convicted of murder following the Whiskey Au Go Go nightclub bombing – the greatest act of mass murder on mainland Australia in the Twentieth Century.

Cats were tolerated at the prison and generations of cats had interbred within the walls producing almost a unique Boggo breed. Some of these cats were "owned" by prisoners and they were quite possessive of their pets. The most famous pet within the walls of the gaol was "Tripod". Many prisoners claimed ownership of Tripod. Many more just loved his company. He was a big tom cat – well fed but tough. He was the top cat in the gaol, the mascot of Number Two Division.

There are a number of versions as to how Tripod got his name. The commonest account is that his leg got caught in a cell door when a prison officer slammed it shut, breaking it. A number of prisoners contributed funds to have Tripod taken to a vet and his leg was amputated. Others say the leg was lost in a riot. In another version, a jealous inmate cut it off to spite another prisoner who claimed ownership of the tom (untrue). The greatest story is that Tripod lost his leg in a battle between himself and the prison's biggest, toughest rat. According to the story:

> Tripod and this rat had hated each other for years. Tripod used to sleep at night on a sandstone ledge under a window just above the ground, absorbing the warmth from the day. One night he deliberately dangled his leg in front of his enemy who took the bait and the leg. Tripod pounced on him and killed him but lost his leg as a consequence.

Dan Fritz, the famous hunger striker of Number Two Division in the 1980s kept Tripod in his cell, F2. They were great mates and Dan got permission to have a small hole cut in the wire mesh in the door to allow Tripod to come and go as he pleased, day or night. When Number Two Division closed in 1989, Dan, close to being paroled, stayed on as caretaker in the now deserted prison. By this time Tripod had died. His body had been buried with a great deal of sorrow by prisoners in the garden in front of the white gates which led into the compound some years before. A small shrub was planted over his grave. At night when Dan was alone he would often stand in the middle of the gaol with his thoughts. On more than one occasion Dan swears he saw Tripod hobble in his distinctive way and stop in the middle of the compound. Around the circular path of the compound all the surviving prison cats would assemble and they would meow to their three-legged leader.

Visitors to the prison swear that an invisible cat has rubbed against them or that they have seen a cat dart out of a cell in one of the cellblocks. The cell it is seen is F2, which, for a time, was Tripods home. Even in death though, Tripod still hobbles.

GHOST STORY

WHERE A GHOST WAS ALWAYS SEEN: The Back Track, Number Two Division where "Casper" lurked
Source: Author's own collection.

Chapter 12

CASPER

Officers on their first night of Back Track duty in Number Two Division would definitely see a ghost.

An older officer would walk new officers out onto the track. On route the old guard would tell the "greenhorn", as new warders were called, of all the stories of ghosts at Boggo Road. The colour would slowly drain from the greenhorn's face.

Suddenly the older guard would stop and grab the new fellow: 'I forgot my fags (cigarettes). You wait here. I'll go get them'.

He would walk away leaving the creeped guard all alone.

Several minutes would pass. Then, a strange noise would be heard – a moan. And then it was seen. A ghost flew up out of a drain beside the track, up the wall and over the top. The greenhorn would turn and run straight back to the main gate where he would run smack into the older guard laughing his head off.

He would lead the new recruit through the small door in the main gate and around to the outside of the wall where the two fellas on night shift in Number One Division would be standing laughing their heads off too.

Earlier in the day a pulley was attached to C Tower across the Track to the sanitation yard fence. A sheet attached to fishing line was set up so that when the guard on compound duty gave it a pull the sheet flew across the track. The "ghost" complete with drawn on eyes and mouth was introduced as "Casper".

A prison officer by the name of Ron Darby was the biggest prankster and was often the one to set the trap for new officers.

The tunnel between One and Two Division was also a likely place for pranks. Above a grate at one end an officer would lie in wait for an unsuspecting officer and then would scream out 'boo'. It was so cold and eerie in the "Tunnel of Love", as it was nicknamed by prisoners, that this sent guards out of their skin in fright.

Jokes weren't limited to guards. A former superintendent in the 1930s like most prison officers in those days used to cycle to work. When he knew that there was a new fellow on duty he'd ride down through the tunnel from Number One Division and out into Two Division. He'd then ride around and around the track, a sheet covering himself and his bike. It isn't hard to imagine in the days of Dracula and Frankenstein a person being terrified as a white object come flying along the track at high speed moaning and groaning.

It is easy to laugh but these pranks only succeeded because the guards were frightened. It was very, very creepy out there.

Many officers walked off the job on their first night, never to return.

THE BACKTRACK OF NUMBER ONE DIVISION: This rare photograph, taken from B Tower on
the wall of Number One Division, shows the Back Track which ran along the inside of the back
wall. This was regarded by warders as being the creepiest place within Boggo Road Gaol. This

Chapter 13

THE GRAVEYARD SHIFT:
TALES OF THE BACK TRACK

The nightshift, known as the "graveyard shift" lasted eight hours, from 10.30pm – 6.30am. It was long and extremely boring. It was also, at times, bloody creepy.

There were some "screws", as the prisoners called guards, who would not do the night shifts. They refused. When rostered on nights they would do anything to swap to a different shift. Some of them went so far as to falsify records – their names appearing on the rosters but they actually didn't show up, having organised another officer to take their place. One officer told me that a mate of his never once in fifteen years as a guard there actually did a single night shift. Records say he did, as did his timesheets, but a packet of tobacco slipped to the right person took care of the details...

Guards tell me that beating fatigue was hard. Every method was tried – officers that smoked would sometimes smoke one after another to get a nicotine hit. Others may have brought a thermos flask of tea or coffee along with them and would drink cup after cup. Some would go for walks down the track to get exercise or jump on the spot. As the night stretched on, the guards would become more and more tired. For some these methods were used to remain alert so they can perform their duties; for others it was more than that. It was to try to prevent tiredness as this brought the ghosties... Once they entered this semi-awake state, the haunting would begin.

* * *

Running around the inside of the wall of both old Number One Division and also Number Two Division was a "no man's land" called the Back Track. Both tracks were regarded as being creepy... but that which ran along the back wall of Number One Division was regarded as being the creepiest place within Boggo Road Gaol.

The Track at Number Two Division was reasonably well lit compared to that of Number One Division. One's Back Track had only a single light at each corner where the wall turned. These old fashioned lights consisted of a tin shade and a single bulb which merely lit up the area directly below. Between each light it was almost pitch black. Torches did little to stop the eerie feeling along this section of track. On one side was the great wall of the prison, on the other, the wooden (and later mesh and barb wired topped) fences that encircled the yards, creating a dark passageway that guards would have to pass through again and again during the night as they patrolled around and around. It was bloody creepy.

Both tracks were covered in fine pea gravel which formed a surface which would create noise in the stillness of the night. Guards on night duty could easily pick out even a slight noise. They often heard noises they could not explain.

On a number of occasions a lone officer patrolling the Back Track at the rear of old Number One Division heard the sound of a whistle being blown. Guards at night carried whistles in the event of an emergency. The guard who heard the sound this night raced to where he thought the noise had come from only to find no fellow officer present. It was like an unseen ghost had summoned him.

Above: PAINTED WALL: The lower part of the wall inside Number Two Division was painted white to end stories of figures being seen in the dark. It only made the apparitions clearer.

Source: Author's own collection

Left: SENTRY BOX: These small wooden structures provided shelter for officers in bad weather. A telephone connected the sentry box to the Gatehouse.

Source: Author's own collection

In 1970 extra patrols were put out on the track after a prison officer saw what he called a big white shapeless mass on top of the dividing wall of an exercise yard in the gaols old Number One Division in the early hours of the morning when he was on a patrol. He claimed it slid off the wall and disappeared into the darkness. The guard reported it to a senior officer and a report of sighting a "ghost" was logged. The spot where he saw the "ghost" was just behind A Wing where the gallows used to be. The prison officer asked for a transfer to Townsville Gaol and never returned to Boggo Road. Over the years, allegedly a number of experienced officers also quit after doing the graveyard shift on the Track.

* * *

In both Divisions warders would see things…dark shapes and shadows, like those cast by people would dart out across the track out of the corner of their eye. Sometimes they would be seen in the extreme distance, clearly visible on the stark white painted wall. In the 1940s, the lower wall inside the Gaol had been painted white to just above the height of a man, to prevent these 'tricks of the light'. This only made the ghostly figures *clearer*.

In the early 1980s a very serious incident occurred. An officer patrolling the track in Number Two Division saw a figure at the far end of the track and actually fired his gun at it. The sound of the shots alerted the entire prison. Within a minute guards with weapons drawn converged at the scene. They found the officer in a state of near hysterics. An internal enquiry was held and as far as can be substantiated it was written up that the officer had fired at a ghost. He was subsequently transferred.

Some of these experiences were quite humorous. Many an officer mistook owls sitting on the wall of the gaol as a prisoner trying to escape. The claws of the bird from a distance would appear as the fingers and hands of a man about to drop himself to freedom, and the body of the owl his head. A change of clothes was almost required when the "escapee" escaped into the air flapping his wing – a real jail bird, not a phantasm.

One officer had a very weird experience. One night, on patrol, Don Walters found a fire hose had seemingly unravelled itself. Such equipment was always kept neat and tidy, ready for use. The strangest part was that the full length of the hose was pointing straight up into the air, like the old Indian rope trick. Don tried to pull it down but it would not budge. Another officer was summoned to witness to the bizarre incident. He too pulled on the hose to no avail. Despite examining every possibility – that it was stuck on something or it was a prank - they could not account for it. Instead, they decided they would keep what happened to themselves rather than endure the heckles of others if they told of it, or be considered mad or worse – unfit – for the job.

The Back Track of Number Two Division was where the officers also claimed a figure used to salute to them - an apparition of a guard which walked the track as if it was doing its rounds. They called this ghost "Bernie" after the warder murdered at the prison. This ghost was friendly, but would target officers who fell asleep or closed their eyes by producing footsteps without a body walking towards them.

A warder named Doug snuck into a sentry box in the early 1980s to read a magazine. These small boxes provided shelter in the event of poor weather. Guards were not permitted however to sit down whilst on duty. If they were caught sitting then it was instant dismissal, even if it was raining. It was extremely quiet. Not a sound. He was deep in concentration reading when he heard footsteps behind him. The sound of footsteps in the gravel. To quote Doug:

> I nearly shit myself. I thought that I had been busted. I jumped up and looked around, looked everywhere but there was no one around.

Seeing things on the walls was common. In the 1980s police too thought that they saw a ghost on the wall of Boggo Road. One night, officers from the Dutton Park police station were taking a break at "Ribbetts" takeaway on Annerley Road, directly across the road from the gaol, when one of them spied a man sitting on the wall of Number Two Div, dangling his legs over the side. Certain of what they saw, the police alerted prison authorities who immediately went into action to prevent an escape. Guards and police swarmed to the spot on the wall where the inmate had been seen, but where now there was nothing. The phantom inmate left nothing but embarrassed police who swore that they had seen what they had seen.

Officer George William Carter regularly did the night-shift on the track at Number Two Division. The reason he did was simple - George had a hard childhood. A married man with a young family in the 1970s, his drive was to give his wife and children a better life than he had growing up in England. Family men were reliable and always willing to do extra shifts to bring home money. Boggo Road needed them. In a time honoured way George got the job through a good friend, Ralph "Dixie" Stein who was already working at Boggo Road Gaol. Ralph was a "pom" too - like a lot of officers at that time.

A tall, fit man, nothing seemed to rattle George. From 1974 to 1991 he worked in the prison system. While their father rarely talked about his work, his children knew what he did when he went off to work each day in his neat, pressed uniform. The family grew up with stories of the infamous Whiskey Au Go Go firebombers, James Finch's claims of innocence and John Stuart swallowing wire crosses. Sometimes George wasn't home for quite a stretch of time. If work colleagues – all "pommy" warders like him - dropped around for a visit or a dinner party they'd hear more stories – tales of night tubs being thrown at officers, rooftop protests, riots, lock-downs. They talked too about a ghost on the track.

George's family often observed the respect their father had in public. Men, former prisoners, would stop and give him a salute as they had inside. Some even shook his hand according to his daughter Sharon who recalled:

> ...people would see Dad in the supermarket, and give a little salute, sort of, you know that hand motion, as they went past him, and you would know that was a "crim", and you would say to Dad, 'Oh, where do you know him from', and he would say 'Oh, from my work', you know, and you knew full well that he had been a prisoner. He was not a bastard "screw".

Despite his job in such a monstrous place, George wrote poetry, keeping a little diary notebook for his shifts in prison, in which he would scribble poems, bringing them home for his wife and children to read. They were pretty good. He wrote purely for fun. "Sylvie Got a Pushbike" written after buying his wife a bicycle is a family classic. He signed every poem G. W. Carter.

George also wrote about Boggo Road Gaol - including one about P.O.G.S., the Prison Officers Golf Society. He and a lot of his warder mates loved their golf, so they formed a club.

In July 1982 he wrote about the ghost of the track in Number Two Division. Then in his thirties he wrote about what it was like to work the Gaol track, waiting for the ghost. His children loved the poem.

> I suppose bored up there at night, with his lunch box with a tube of condensed milk in it (that us kids used to love to get our hands on) that's where a poem like this came from.

It seems unlikely George actually ever saw the ghost. According to his daughter he would have made a bigger deal out of it if he had:

> I think it was a bit tongue in cheek of Dad... we always thought it was pretty funny that Dad would spend his nights in the dark, you know, and they were armed, and we used to say to him, 'What do you do up there all night?' and he says, 'Just watch for things, and hope you didn't see the ghost', you know?

Left: OFFICER G. W. CARTER: George William Carter, who penned a poem about the ghost of the track inside Number Two Division.
Source: Carter family

While George Carter passed away in 2002, aged 66 years, his handwritten poetry survives, cherished by his wife and three children. Thanks to them we reproduce his vivid poem, "Two Track", about the ghost of the backtrack...

TWO TRACK

I was on the track the other night
and feeling kind of low.
Wishing it were half past five
and nearly time to go.....

When I heard footsteps approaching me
and, changing my position,
I saw to my astonishment,
a ghostly apparition.......

An officer I thought it were
In raincoat long and black,
walking o so slowly
along that gravel track......

I stood there, frozen to the spot,
blood pounding in my head,
as that pallid face came toward me,
my body shook with dread.

I could hear the rustle of his clothes
I could hear his steady breath
But no mortal man could own those eyes,
those cold grey eyes of death.

He never faltered in his stride,
that slow and measured gait,
until he reached the tower,
where he stopped as if to wait.

I gazed in wonder and in awe
as he reached into his pocket
and saw him glance at a pocket watch
with roman numerals on it.

He turned just then and looked at me
My chest went tight with pain
And slow and clear he said to me
"Bloody late relief again"

G. W. Coates.

MAP – BOGGO ROAD GAOL

Below are sites relating to the stories referred to in this book:

BOGGO ROAD GAOL
NUMBER TWO DIVISION

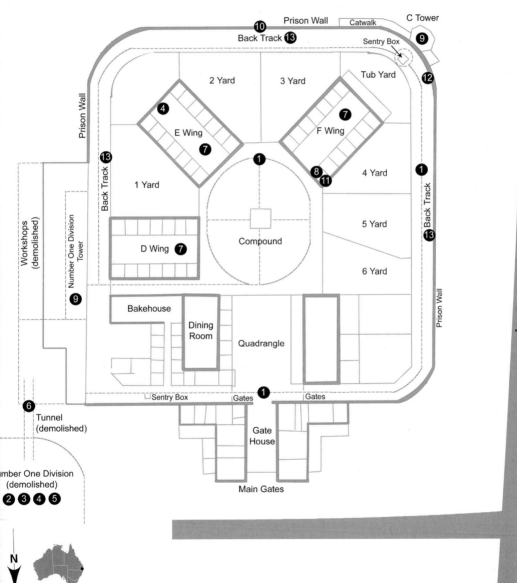

GHOST TRAIL

Below are some of the historic locations referred to in this book:

1 *THE WARDER OF NUMBER TWO DIVISION*

Location: NUMBER TWO DIVISION,
ANNERLEY ROAD, DUTTON PARK

2 *THE GALLOWS*

Location: NUMBER ONE DIVISION (DEMOLISHED)

3 *THE HAUNTED HANGMAN*

Location: NUMBER ONE DIVISION (DEMOLISHED)

4 *A BANSHEE WAILED –
THE LAST MAN HANGED*

Location: NUMBER ONE & TWO DIVISION,
ANNERLEY ROAD, DUTTON PARK

5 *THE GRAVES*

Location: NUMBER ONE DIVISION (DEMOLISHED)

6 *THE TUNNEL OF LOVE*

Location: NUMBER ONE DIVISION (DEMOLISHED)

7 THE CELLS

Location: D,E,F WING CELLBLOCKS -
NUMBER TWO DIVISION,
ANNERLEY ROAD, DUTTON PARK

8 CELL F2

Location: F WING CELLBLOCK -
NUMBER TWO DIVISION,
ANNERLEY ROAD, DUTTON PARK

9 THE TOWERS

Location: C TOWER -
NUMBER TWO DIVISION,
ANNERLEY ROAD, DUTTON PARK

10 THE CEMETERY FOG

Location: SOUTHERN WALL -
NUMBER TWO DIVISION,
ANNERLEY ROAD, DUTTON PARK

11 TRIPOD THE GHOST CAT

Location: NUMBER TWO DIVISION,
ANNERLEY ROAD, DUTTON PARK

12 CASPER

Location: BACKTRACK -
NUMBER TWO DIVISION,
ANNERLEY ROAD, DUTTON PARK

13 THE GRAVEYARD SHIFT:
TALES OF THE BACK TRACK

Location: BACKTRACK -
NUMBER ONE AND TWO DIVISION,
ANNERLEY ROAD, DUTTON PARK

REFERENCES

Chapters 1 -13

Various personal oral histories (withheld by request).
Author's own collection.

Chapter 2

The Truth, Sunday, 23 July 1905, page 5;
The Truth, Sunday, 20 May 1906, page 5;

Chapter 3

The Truth, Sunday, 19 November 1905, page 5;

ABOUT THE AUTHOR

Jack Sim, Australian Ghost Hunter, searching for more haunted sites to join his *Ghost Trails* series.

Brisbane's infamous "man in black", Jack Sim, walks the shadowy streets of town in search of stories and tales of horrible history. Sim has long been fascinated by stories of the past, especially crime stories, ghost tales and jail birds. Jack is often seen late at night driving his 1939 Studebaker President eighteen foot long straight-eight hearse in search of new material.

Jack Sim has dedicated his life to preserving the details of things and subjects that all of us find both macabre and thrilling. He is the publisher of the *Classic Crime, Murder Trails, Ghost Trails* and *the Boggo Road Gaol* Series. Over the past 5 years he has published 12 titles under these series, including HAUNTED BRISBANE: *Ghosts of the River City,* THE GHOSTS OF TOOWONG CEMETERY: *Brisbane's Necropolis* and ESCAPE *From Boggo Road Gaol Vol. 1.*

Since last century Jack Sim has become an almost iconic character in Southern Queensland, undertaking his eerie Ghost Tours and Crime & Murder Tours, with a collection of other hosts, of the region's most haunted sites, such as Boggo Road Gaol, Toowong Cemetery and Dutton Park Cemetery. His work promoting history and heritage to visitors and locals has been seen in national and international media and documentaries such as Getaway, Extra, and the Seven Network's Great South East. He has strived to gain greater recognition for the value of storytelling and oral history and he has been the longest running operator of ghost tours on mainland Australia. Visit www. ghost-tours.com.au & www.crimetours.com.au

Jack Sim has also earned himself many fans as a guest on the Paranormal Panel with Tino Pezzimenti from UFO Research Queensland discussing all things paranormal as well as Crime at Nine on Walter William's evening radio show on 4BC (1116am), where he discusses true crime, from Brisbane and international history, some infamous, others long forgotten. Jack also has worked hard to promote tourism in Queensland; Tony Robinson, well known British TV personality, visited Australia in 2012 and filmed an episode of his "Walks" series in the Sunshine State, thanks to Jack's initiative.

Jack Sim is proud of the support his businesses have given the historical community through donations of his time and money. The Haunted Heritage fund of his company Ghost Tours Pty Ltd restored the vandalised Piper Memorial in partnership with Ipswich City Council in 2010. Visit www.hauntedheritage.com.au

Join this dark historian as he strives to undertake us on a journey to the unpleasant side of society, that no-one knew existed or wanted to.

BUY A BOOK OR UNDERTAKE A TOUR... or else. Visit www.jacksim.com.au

OTHER TITLES

GHOST TRAILS
Series

HAUNTED PLACES

HAUNTED SITES

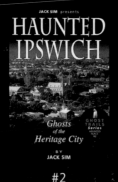

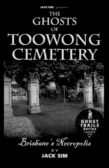

#1

#2

#1

#2

For information about current and forthcoming Ghost Trails titles contact the publisher:

JACK SIM PUBLICATIONS

PO Box 1457, Sunnybank Hills Brisbane Queensland Australia 4109

Tel: +61 7 3344 7264 Email: orders@jacksim.com.au

www.ghosttrails.com.au

TOUR DETAILS

To undertake a Ghost Tour of this haunted site visit...